THIS BOOK BELONGS TO THE AMAZING:

Expert Builder

TO all the creators, artists, inventors, daydreamers and imagination users
who fill the world with magic.

and Theo, Sonny and Meena

History

The Scrap Kins came from a love of drawing and making things.
The characters are based on my own childhood monster creations.

Have a great idea for a project? Want The Scrap Kins to visit your school?
We'd love to hear your comments, suggestions and ideas.
Contact: brian@thescrapkins.com

Thanks for your support.

Brian Yanish, / Scrap Kins creator

Published by Crackle Press, New York

SCRAP KINS is a registered Trademark of Brian Yanish.

ISBN-13: 978-0615438948 (Crackle Press)
ISBN-10: 0615438946

www.thescrapkins.com

Scrap Project

Itcher's Tube Tiger

What You'll Need:

- 1 Toilet paper tube
- or a Paper Towel Tube cut in half
- Scissors
- Markers or Crayons

1 Make 3 small cuts in the bottom of your tube about three fingers apart.

Ask an adult to help you cut anything difficult.

2 Fold up the two flaps to form your tiger's feet

3 Cut out a few triangle shapes to form claws.

4 Turn your tube around and cut off the extra piece behind the feet.

5 Cut this piece in half to make your tiger's arms.

6 Cut a piece out of the front of your tube to make the head.

7 Cut 2 small slits behind the ears.

Turn your tube around and cut off the extra piece behind the ears.

8 Round the end of this piece to make your tail.

9 Cut a small slit in the back and insert your tail!

10 Make the slits behind the ears longer for arms.

11 Insert your arms!

12 Use markers, crayons or paints to decorate. Draw a face and stripes.

YOU'VE GOT A TUBE TIGER! GRRRRRRR!

Find more crafts online

www.thescrapkins.com

SCRAP KINS

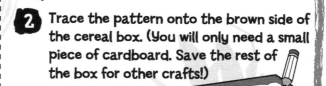

Digger's Page Peeker Bookmark

Make It!

HEAD

FOLDING LINE

BODY

PATTERN

"Oookery Bookery!"
In Digger-talk that means. "I love books."

---

1 Carefully cut out the pattern with scissors.

2 Trace the pattern onto the brown side of the cereal box. (You will only need a small piece of cardboard. Save the rest of the box for other crafts!)

3 Cut out the cardboard with scissors.

HEAD

4 Fold down the top (HEAD) piece of your bookmark along the folding line. Make sure the brown side of the cardboard is on the outside.

5 Draw or paint your Scrap Kin's face and body on the brown side of the bookmark. Be creative! Your Scrap Kin can have as many eyes as you want or whatever crazy body you can dream up.

6 Give your Scrap Kin a home in your favorite book!

What You'll Need:

Cereal Box
or other thin cardboard

Scissors

Pencil

Markers or Crayons or Paints

Scrap Kins

Scrap Project

Floatable Milk Carton Pirate Ship

Make It!

What You'll Need:

- **MILK** — milk or juice carton (any size)
- toilet paper tube
- egg carton
- scissors
- 2 drinking straws
- hole puncher
- stapler
- cork
- GLUE
- pencil & markers
- tape
- small piece of cardboard
- 2 buttons

Ask for help from an adult before starting your boat.

1 Cut the top of your milk carton off.

2 Turn the top piece over and put it inside the bottom piece. Secure with staples.

3 Cut out the side windows (called "gunports") for your cannon. Fold down the flaps.

4 Put up the main mast. Carefully poke a hole through the floor of the ship. Push the end of the straw into the hole.

You can wrap a piece of tape around the end of the straw so it stands tight in the hole.

5 Make your sail.

Cut open the toilet paper tube. (Fold it back to help it stay open.)

Draw and decorate your sail.

Punch 2 holes through the sail.

Slide it onto the mast. (Use tape to secure.)

6 Add details to your ship.

Cut the other straw into 1 long piece and 1 short.

Fit the long piece of straw into the front of the ship.

This is called the "bowsprit."

Cut 1 cup from the bottom of an egg carton. Poke a hole in the bottom and slide it onto the top of the mast. This is called the "Crow's Nest."

Cut a small rectangle of cardboard for your flag. Use the small piece of straw as the flagpole. Make a small cut in the straw, slide in the edge of the flag and tape the back.

You can tuck the flagpole between the 2 edges of the ship.

7 Build your cannon.

Glue the buttons to both sides of the cork.

Captain Cork

You can use another cork to make your ship's captain. Make a hat from cardboard and draw a face.

8 Launch your ship! It's ready to sail the Seven Seas!

www.thescrapkins.com

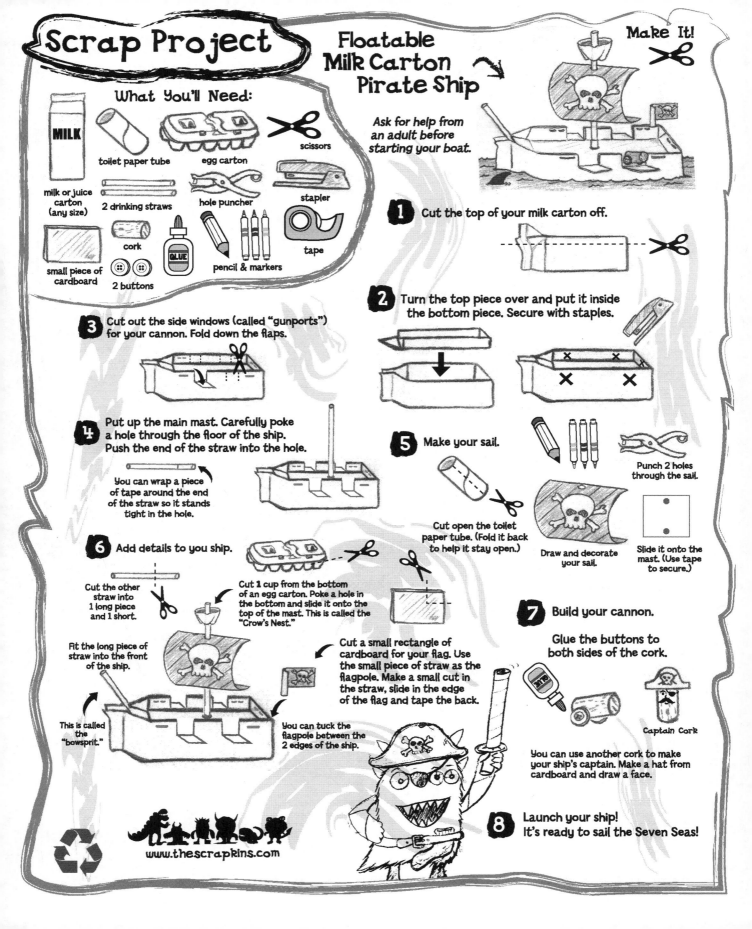

Best Filthy Friends

B.f.f.s

Draw Your own Scrap Kin here.

SCRAP KINS®

Mini Jean Tote Bag

Make It!

What You'll Need:

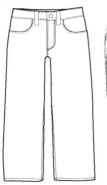

1 Pair of Jeans
(any size will do)

Scissors

FABRIC glue

3 Binder clips
or clothespins
(large paper clips will
also work)

Buttons, fabric paint or
other stuff to decorate
your tote

1 Cut Leg **A** across from seam to seam. Make the height of your tote around 9 inches. You should be able to make 2-3 tote bags from an average size kid's pair of jeans. (More if you use adult jeans.)

2 Cut off side seams from Leg **B**.

3 Cut 3 thin strips up the length of Leg **B** for your handle. Make each strip about as wide as your thumb. (You'll need 3 strips for each handle if you make more than 1 bag.)

4 Put the 3 strips on top of each other and fold down about 3 inches. Clip together your 3 strips with a Binder Clip or clothespin. (If you don't have that you could tie them together with string or use a safety pin.)

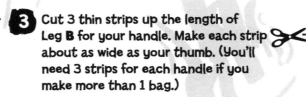

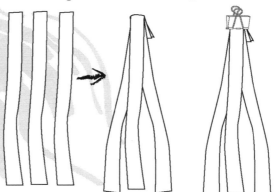

5 Braid your strips together to make your tote bag handle.

How to Braid:

*Remember: You always fold over the middle strip every time.

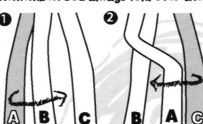

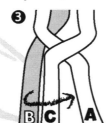

❶ To start, Strip B is the middle. Grab Strip A and bring it over Strip B.

❷ Now Strip A is the middle. Grab Strip C and bring it over Strip A.

❸ Now Strip C is the middle. Grab Strip B and bring it over Strip C. Now B is the middle. Repeat steps.

TIPS:

*It helps to hold the strips between your thumb and 1st finger. Use your other hand to move the free strip.

*To get a smaller braid keep the strips tight and pull upward to tighten.

ScrapKins®

Mini Jean Tote Bag - PART 2

 Make It!

6

Carefully cut a small hole using scissors at the top center of your tote.
* If you need help ask an adult.

FLIP over your tote and make a hole at the same spot on the other side.

How to cut a hole safely:

"Pinch & Snip"

Bunch up the material at the spot you want your hole so it forms a little hill.

Snip across the very top of the hill to make your hole!

7

Glue together the edges of your tote along the bottom using fabric glue. Place 3 clips along the edge to hold your tote while the glue dries.

Let the Glue dry overnight before you take off clips. You can still decorate your bag while the clips are on.

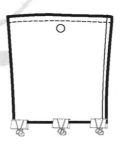

8

Gather the strips at one end of your handle.
Push through the hole in your tote from the outside.
Pull ends inside until you have enough room to tie 2 knots.

• First tie 2 of the strip ends together in a knot.
• Next, tie another knot with the free strip end.
• Repeat steps on the other side.

9

Decorate your tote!
Try using other recyclables that you can glue in a design. You can also use fabric paint.

Be Green. Be Creative!

 **SCRAP KINS®**

"Mother of INVENTION"

Swooper is working on a plan to protect Scrap City from being discovered.

Scrap Kins®

Swooper's Recycle Robot

Swooper needs to build a watch-robot to help protect Scrap City. Follow her plans to build your own robot from recyclables found at home!

If you need help, ask an adult before starting your Robot.

What You'll Need:

- Piece of thin cardboard (cereal box or tissue box works best)
- Small Juice or Milk carton (14 Fluid Oz works best)
- Toilet paper tube
- drinking straw
- Tape
- hole puncher
- Rubber Band
- GLUE
- Scissors
- Stapler
- Pencil
- Markers or Crayons or paints

1 Trace two circles onto cardboard using your toiletpaper tube as a guide. Cut them out and punch a hole in the middle.

2 Flatten toilet paper tube and carefully cut in half with scissors.
Cut one of the pieces in half again.
These are your **wheels**.

3 Insert cardboard circles inside your wheels. They should fit very tight. You can trim them a bit with scissors but keep them tight. It's okay to have the circle edges bend.
Glue around the BACK edge of each circle.
Set aside to dry.

4 Open the flaps of you carton all the way.
Carefully cut along the diagonal side seams at the top opening on both sides.
Fold out the triangular arms.

5 Trace the bottom of your carton onto cardboard for a robot **face-plate**. Draw a larger rectangle for a **chest plate** for the front of your robot.
Cut them out and decorate. Draw your robot's face and chest. Be creative!

6 **Get help from an adult** to staple together the top flaps of your carton. Use another staple to secure your **face-plate** to the front flap.

7 Glue your chest plate to the front of the body. Use a rubber band to hold it in place until dry.

8 **Get help from an adult** to poke a hole straight through both sides of the carton. Use a pencil and poke hole at bottom center of carton.
Push straw all the way through both holes.

9 Gently push your wheels onto the straws on both sides.
Wrap a tiny piece of tape around the straw to hold the wheels on.
Trim extra straw with scissors.

YOU'RE DONE!

Find more Recycled Art projects online

www.scrapkins.com

U Do It!

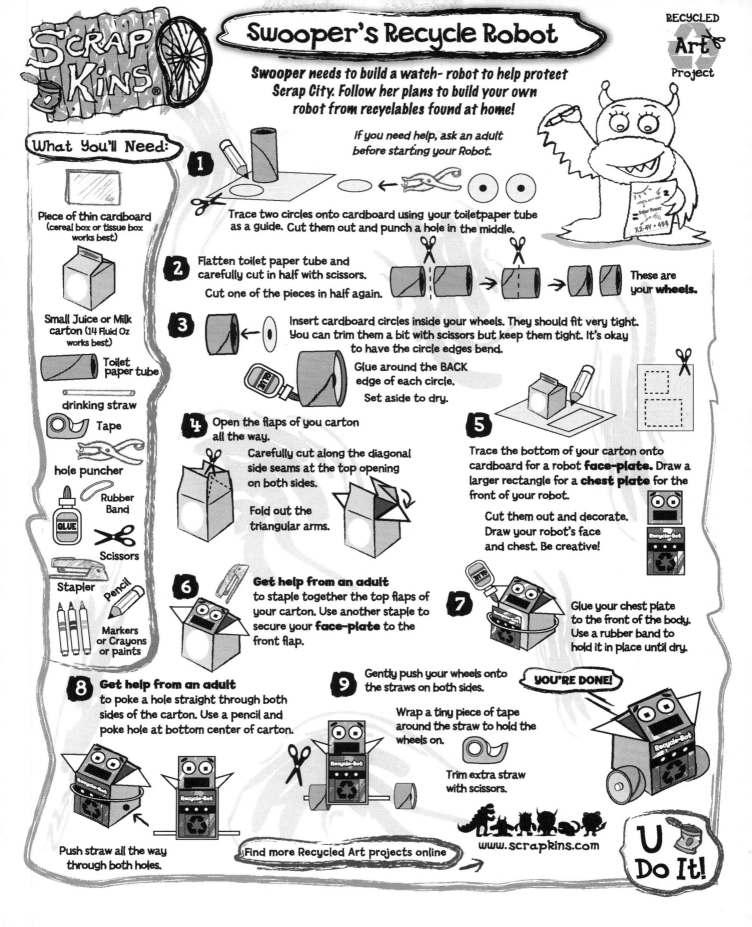

Chomper's Foam Glider

Chomper figured out how to turn an old styrofoam tray into a flying glider. Follow his plans to build your own!

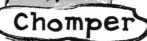

What You'll Need:

Styrofoam Deli or Produce Tray

2 Paper Clips

Stickers

Scissors

Tape

Pencil

Markers or Crayons or paints

1 Print out the Patterns and trace the plane parts on to the back of your foam tray. (It's easier to use a marker.)

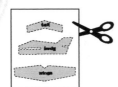

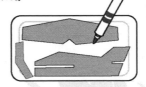

Chomper

2 Carefully cut out the parts with scissors.

wings

tail

body

3 Slide the wings into the front slot.

Slide the tail into the back slot.

4 Design & Decorate your plane with paints, markers & stickers.

5 Put a piece of tape on both sides of the front slot.

Green Machine

6 Slide 1 or 2 paper clips on the front (Nose) of the plane for weight.

Green Machine

YOU'RE READY TO FLY!

EXTRA: Have a contest to see how far or fast you plane can go. Experiment with different body, wing and tail shapes to see how it changes the plane's performance.

Find more Recycled Art projects online

www.scrapkins.com

U Do It!

Chomper's Foam Glider

Carefully cut out with scissors and trace onto your foam tray.

PLANE PATTERNS

tail

body

wings

Snowy Owl Milk Carton Bird Feeder

PATTERN for TALONS

(Cut out and trace.)

Snowy Owl Milk Carton Bird Feeder

Follow Swooper's Instructions to make your very own bird feeder.
Ask an adult for help before starting. *Be creative & have fun!*

What You'll Need:

- Piece of thin cardboard (cereal box or tissue box works best)
- 1 Clean Half Gallon or Quart Size Milk or Juice Carton
- 1 Paper Clip
- 2 Drinking Straws
- 15 Inches of fishing line or string
- 1 cup of birdseed
- Waterproof Paints & Brushes
- Markers
- Pencil
- Scissors
- GLUE
- Stapler
- hole punch

1 Draw an arch shape on the front of your carton. (If your carton is open at the top use a stapler to staple it closed.)

2 Use a pencil to carefully poke a hole at the top of your arch and insert scissor tip. Cut out arch and save for later.

3 Draw a rectangle shape on the side of carton for your wing. Leave the top edge open. **Repeat on opposite side.**

4

WINGS
Carefully cut the 3 sides of your rectangle on both sides and bend out your wings.

Cut off the back corner to round out wing.

5

TAIL
Draw a rectangle on back of carton. Leave the bottom edge open.

Cut out rectangle and fold down tail. Trim corners to round out tail.

6

TALONS
Cut out the talon pattern from **previous page** and trace onto the arch shape you saved. Trace and cut out 2 talons. (If you lose your arch use cardboard.)

7 Put glue on the back half of talons and stick under front bottom edge of carton. **TIP:** Glue will stick better if you scratch the back half of talon and carton bottom with a scissor edge.

8

EYES and BEAK
Draw 2 circles for eyes and a diamond for a beak on cardboard. Cut out with scissors.

9 Glue eyes to top of carton. Glue beak so its bottom edge hangs over edge.

10

WING PERCH
Insert 1 straw end into other tightly to form perch.

Punch a hole at the end tip of each wing. Fold up each wing and punch another hole through wing and the side of carton.

Thread your straw perch through hole at wing tip, pass through body and out the other wing tip hole.

11

Decorate your Owl!
Paint the eyes yellow and beak black. Paint the whole body, wings and feet white. Add small blackwave shapes on the wings, back and body front below chin for feather markings. Add some black speckles on top of head. Pupils, nostrils and claws are black.

12 Punch a hole in top of feeder. Bend a paper clip to form a hook and tie fishing line to hole & end of hook. Poke 3 holes in bottom of feeder for drainage. Add your birdseed and hang from a tree or window. **Count & keep track of all your Bird Visitors!**

BIRDFACT!
Snowy Owls are the largest owls in North America. They grow up to 23 inches tall and their wingspan can measure more than four feet.

www.thescrapkins.com

Find more crafts online.

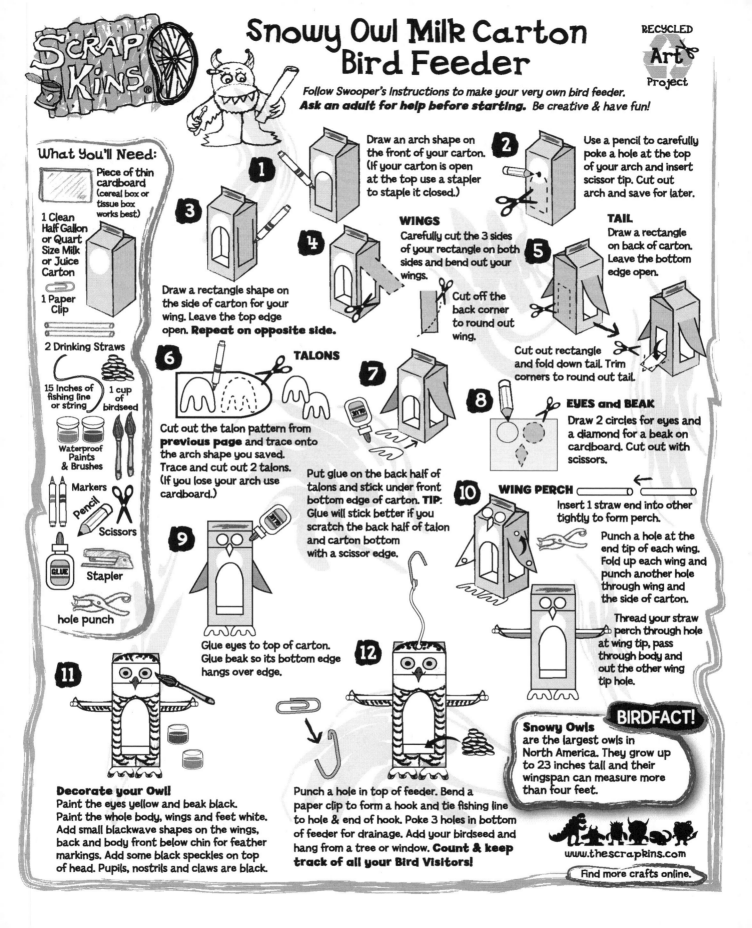

ScrapKins

Itcher's Sock-Pile Search

Itcher's laundry cave is a mess! He's lost his favorite things inside a giant pile of smelly socks.

CAN YOU FIND THESE WORDS?

- UNDERWEAR
- CAN
- TEE SHIRT
- COMIC BOOK
- PIZZA
- HAT
- GUMBALL
- BOX
- TUBESOCK
- BOTTLE
- SNEAKER

Find more FUN online!

www.thescrapkins.com

Words can be up, down, backwards and diagonal. GOOD LUCK!

```
C B O T T L E Q R K
T U T Z Z A C E Q O
E B N D O T K P C O
E L X D B A F I A B
S B T E E X H Z N C
H D X N O R F Z O I
I O S B O T W A O M
R B F H A T F E O O
T U B E S O C K A C
C L L A B M U G O R
```

"The Garden of EATEN"

Stacker is collecting plastic bottles for a new garden.

Stacker daydreams about perfect plants.

Stacker's Bottle Garden

Stacker is getting organized and turning recyclables into a mini garden for his window. Follow his plans to build your own garden!

What You'll Need:

Piece of thin cardboard
(cereal box or tissue box works best)

Plastic water bottle
(thinner plastic bottles are best)

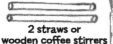

Toilet paper tube

2 straws or wooden coffee stirrers

Any kind of flower or plant seeds

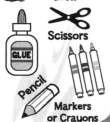

Enough potting soil or dirt to fill half your bottle

Scissors

GLUE

Pencil

Markers or Crayons

1 **Ask an adult** to help you cut the top off your plastic bottle using scissors. Squeeze the bottle to a flatter shape to make cutting easier.

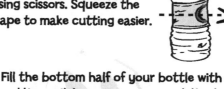

2  Fill the bottom half of your bottle with potting soil. Leave some room at the top.

Poke a small hole in the soil with your finger. Place 2-3 seeds in the hole and cover.

3 Draw a tree-top shape onto your cardboard piece and cut out with scissors. You can also draw a bird.

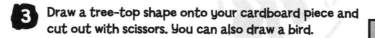

4 Color and decorate your bird and tree-top. You can write your name on the tree-top if you like.

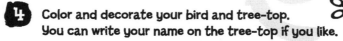

Make tiny snips in the top of your toilet paper tube. Slide your tree top into the slits.

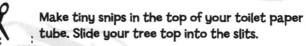

Pinch the tube and make a tiny snip into the side. Poke your straw or coffee stirrer through the hole and snip off to make your tree branch. Glue or tape your bird onto the branch.

5 Draw a flower shape onto your cardboard piece and cut out with scissors.

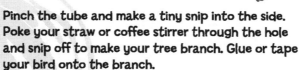

Color your flower. You can cut another small circle for the flower center and glue it into place.

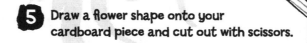

6 Make a tiny cut into the other straw at the top. Slip your flower head into the straw.

7 **Set up your garden.**
Place your flower in the top of the bottle like a vase.

Water your seeds once a week and watch them grow!

EXTRA: Try adding a rock to your garden or play around with extra trees and decorations. Have fun!

www.scrapkins.com

U Do It!

Find more Recycled Art projects online

Scrap Project

Itcher Paper Plate Mask

What You'll Need:

- 1 Paper Plate
- scissors
- tape
- string or rubber band
- Cereal Box or other thin cardboard
- pencil & markers or crayons

1 Carefully cut-out Eye Pattern, Mouth Pattern, & Horn Patterns.

2 Trace Eyes and Mouth on your plate using a pencil.

3 Cut-out Mouth hole from plate. If you need help ask an adult.

4 Cut-out TEETH from Mouth Pattern. Trace 5 Little Horns and 2 Big Horns onto a cereal box and cut them out.

5 Carefully use scissors to cut 4 eye holes. If you need help ask an adult. Cut off a piece two fingers wide from the sides and bottom of plate as shown.

6 Flip over plate and tape Teeth into mouth hole. Tape Horns at top.

7 Carefully cut 2 small holes on sides of mask. Thread one end of string through a hole and tie a knot at the end. Hold mask up to your face. Wrap string around the back of head to measure how much string you will need to make it tight. Cut string, thread through other hole and tie off with a knot.

8 Draw Itcher's eyeball lines and eyebrows. Snip some small lines into side of mask to look like hair. Color and decorate.

YOU'RE ITCHER! GO COLLECT SOME DIRTY SOCKS!

Find more projects online:
www.thescrapkins.com

How to cut safely: "Pinch & Snip"

Here's a good way to safely cut-out shapes from the middle of your plate:

Gently pinch the plate so it folds a bit.

Using your scissors, snip across the fold.

Now you can flatten the plate and put the scissors into the snip to finish cutting.

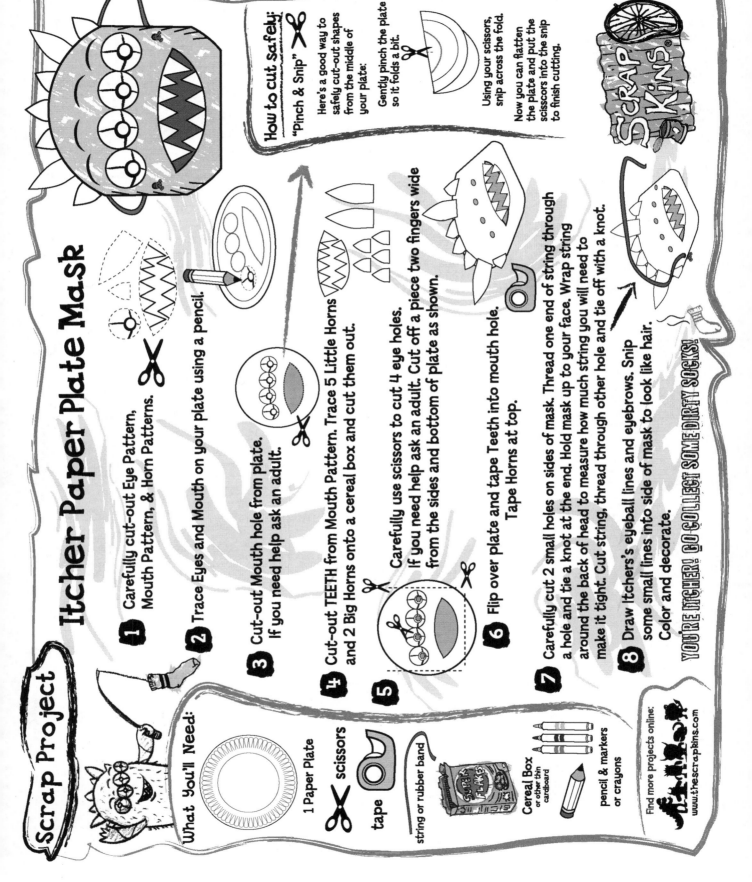

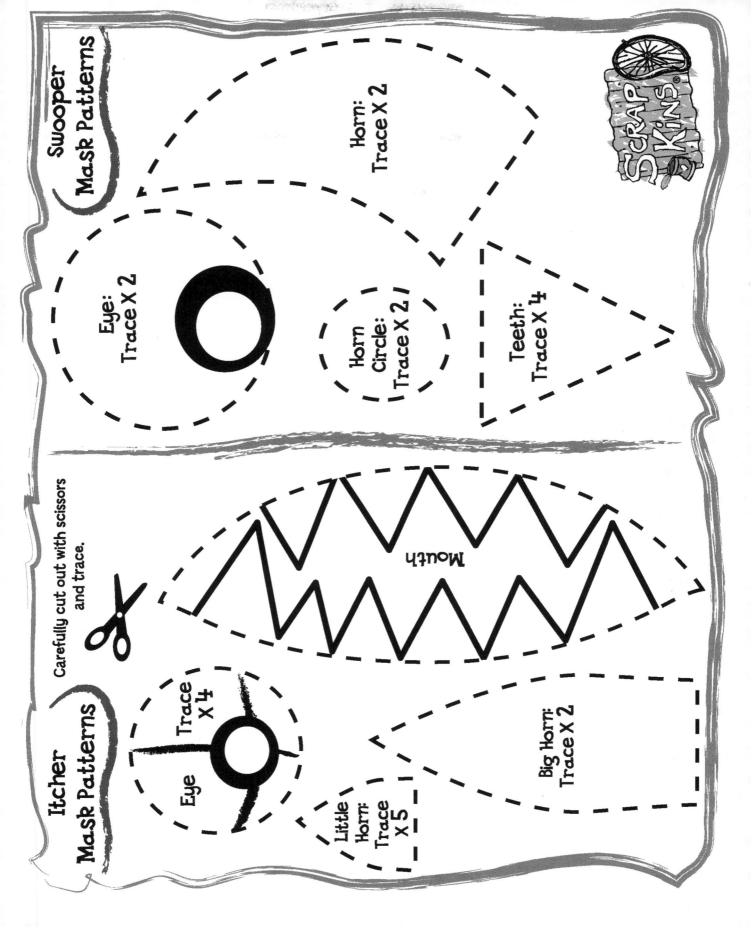

Scrap Project

Swooper Paper Plate Mask

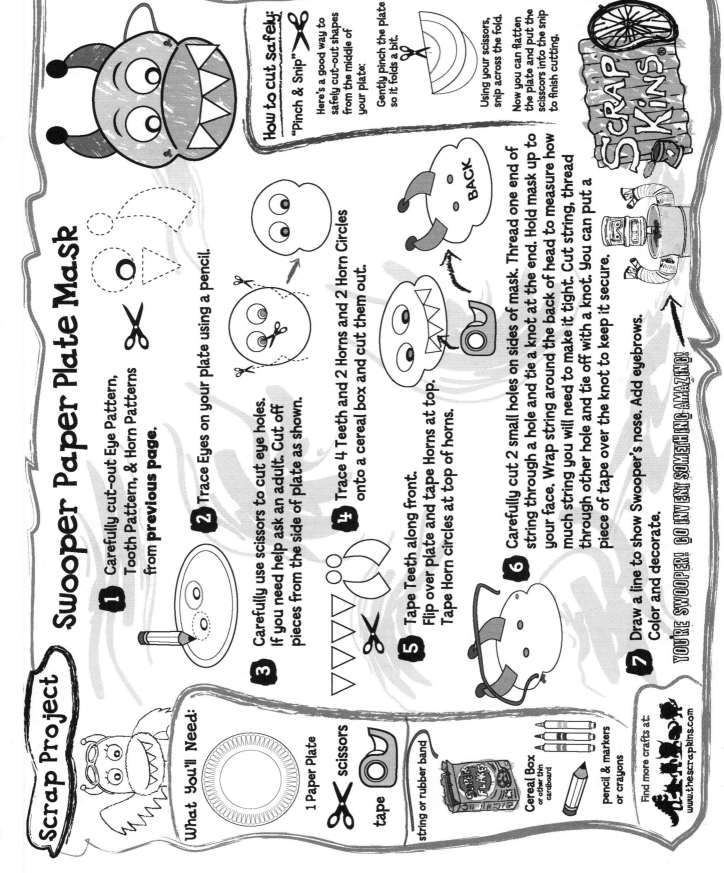

What You'll Need:

1 Paper Plate

scissors

tape

string or rubber band

Cereal Box or other thin cardboard

pencil & markers or crayons

Find more crafts at:
www.thescrapkins.com

How to cut safely: "Pinch & Snip"

Here's a good way to safely cut-out shapes from the middle of your plate:

Gently pinch the plate so it folds a bit.

Using your scissors, snip across the fold.

Now you can flatten the plate and put the scissors into the snip to finish cutting.

1. Carefully cut-out Eye Pattern, Tooth Pattern, & Horn Patterns from **previous page.**

2. Trace Eyes on your plate using a pencil.

3. Carefully use scissors to cut eye holes. If you need help ask an adult. Cut off pieces from the side of plate as shown.

4. Trace 4 Teeth and 2 Horns and 2 Horn Circles onto a cereal box and cut them out.

5. Tape Teeth along front. Flip over plate and tape Horns at top. Tape Horn circles at top of horns.

6. Carefully cut 2 small holes on sides of mask. Thread one end of string through a hole and tie a knot at the end. Hold mask up to your face. Wrap string around the back of head to measure how much string you will need to make it tight. Cut string, thread through other hole and tie it off with a knot. You can put a piece of tape over the knot to keep it secure.

7. Draw a line to show Swooper's nose. Add eyebrows. Color and decorate.

BACK

YOU'RE SWOOPER! GO INVENT SOMETHING AMAZING!

"FIRE HAZARD"

Wrecks finishes welding his "Tower of Cola" sculpture.

What do I make next?

Sometimes an idea finds you...

COMIC PAC

CAT RUN

BOOM!

GHOST BUDDIES

I can't scare.

I can use the things I have to make...

JUNK BOY!

by Wrecks

MY OWN COMIC BOOK!

ACHOO!

Wrecks's Cereal Box Comic Book

Wrecks is making his own comic books out of recycled materials to start a BookStore in Scrap City. Follow the instructions to make your own comic book!

What You'll Need:

Cereal Box (or other thin piece of cardboard you can fold)

Pencil

3-4 sheets of paper

Scissors

Markers, Crayons or Colored Pencils

Stapler

1 Using scissors carefully cut off the front side of a cereal box. (Save the rest of the box for another comic.)

2 Fold your cardboard piece in half so it looks like a little book. Make sure the cereal box pictures are on the inside. Trim the cardboard to whatever size you want your comic to be.

3 Stack 3-4 sheets of paper neatly and fold the stack in half. (Remember: The more paper you use the longer your comic will be.)

cover   inside pages

Trim the edges of the stack to fit inside your cardboard cover.

4 **Ask an adult** to help you staple your pages inside your cover.

cover

5 **Let the creativity begin!**
Come up with a funny or serious Title for your story. Decorate the outside cover of your comic and write your story and draw pictures on the inside.

You may want to draw boxes on your pages like a real comic book to give you spaces to draw.

Write & Draw Your Own Scrap Kins Story

Turn the page to learn how to draw The Scrapkins.

Here are some Story ideas to help get you started:

- What kind of adventure could The Scrap Kins go on?
- What objects do they find at the recycling center?
- What holidays do they celebrate in Scrap City?
- What amazing machine do they build together?
- How do The Scrap Kins help protect the Earth?

www.thescrapkins.com

U Do It!

Find more Recycled Art projects online

How to Draw WRECKS

How to Draw ITCHER

www.thescrapkins.com

How to Draw SWOOPER

How to Draw STACKER

www.thescrapkins.com

Certificate of Master Creativity

For outstanding use of recycled materials, trying new things and thinking like a genius.

Name: _____

Age: _____

Date: _____

Number of projects completed: _____

Presented by Wrecks and Swooper, master artist-builders, Scrap City.

SCRAP SKiNS®

www.thescrapkins.com

Made in the USA
San Bernardino, CA
09 November 2015